H.M. QUEEN ELIZABETH
THE QUEEN MOTHER

A Celebration of Ninety Years

H.M. QUEEN ELIZABETH
THE QUEEN MOTHER

A Celebration of Ninety Years

Tom Corby

NEW ENGLISH LIBRARY

Copyright © 1990 by Tom Corby

Book design by Trevor and Jacqui Vincent

First published in Great Britain in 1990 by
New English Library, Mill Road, Dunton Green, Sevenoaks, Kent.
Editorial office: 47 Bedford Square, London WC1B 3DP.

Typeset by Rowland Phototypesetting Limited, Bury St Edmunds, Suffolk.
Printed in Great Britain by Butler and Tanner Limited, Frome and London.

British Library Cataloguing in Publication Data
Corby, Tom
HM Queen Elizabeth, the Queen Mother.
1. Great Britain. Elizabeth, Queen, Consort of George VI, King of Great Britain
I. Title   941.084092

ISBN 0-450-52535-X

Contents

LEFT *Prince Paul of Serbia commissioned this portrait of Lady Elizabeth
from John Singer Sargent, RA, in April 1923 as a wedding gift to her.
In October that year the newly wed Duke and Duchess of York represented the royal family
in Belgrade at Prince Paul's marriage to Princess Olga of Greece, whose sister Marina,
eleven years later, married Prince George, youngest son of George V and Queen Mary.*

FRONTISPIECE
*An eightieth birthday portrait at Royal Lodge, Windsor,
her weekend retreat when in London. The Queen Mother wears her favourite
blue and her 'trademark' triple strand of pearls.*

Photographic Acknowledgements

The author and publisher are grateful to the following for permission to reproduce their photographs:

CAMERA PRESS pp. 2, 12, 20, 26, 34, 35, 40, 41, 42, 43, 50, 51, 52, 54, 55, 64, 65, 71 *above*, 74, 78, 79, 81, 96, 101, 107, 125, 128, 129, 130, 137, 138, 140, 141, 142
COLORIFIC p. 8
FOX PHOTOS pp. 59, 102, 103, 104, 105, 109, 112, 113, 121
JOE FRIEDMAN p. 23
HULTON-DEUTSCH COLLECTION pp. 53, 68–9, 94, 95, 106, 114, 122, 124
JS LIBRARY p. 139
POPPERFOTO pp. 11, 13, 14, 15, 16, 17, 27, 30, 36, 48, 49, 60, 61, 62, 63, 66, 67, 72, 75, 82, 83, 84, 90, 91, 92, 111
PRESS ASSOCIATION pp. 4, 18, 19, 24, 25, 28, 29, 31, 32, 33, 37, 38 *above and below*, 39, 44, 47, 56, 70, 71 *below*, 73, 76, 77, 80, 87, 93, 97, 98, 99, 100, 110, 116, 118, 119, 123, 131, 133, 134, 135, 136, 143
SYNDICATION INTERNATIONAL pp. 88–9, 108, 115, 117 *above and below*, 120, 126, 127, 132, 144

Acknowledgements

I am grateful to the Queen Mother's Private Secretary, Lieutenant Colonel Sir Martin Gilliat, and other members of Her Majesty's Household, for their willing and generous assistance.

I would also like to thank the staff of the News and Picture Libraries of the Press Association for their patient help in my researches; Anne-Marie Ehrlich, who so diligently carried out the picture research, Trevor Vincent, the designer of this book; Margaret Body, its editor, and Clare Bristow, Publisher of New English Library, for their expert help, encouragement and guidance.

Of my source references I must mention the meticulously researched and detailed biography, written with the authority of its subject, *Queen Elizabeth the Queen Mother* by Dorothy Laird, and the scholarship of other biographers on which I have drawn: Anthony Holden (*The Queen Mother – a Birthday Tribute*), Patrick Howarth (*George VI*), Godfrey Talbot (*The Country Life Book of Queen Elizabeth the Queen Mother*), and Michael Thornton (*Royal Feud*). I also cannot fail to acknowledge the work of Leslie Field (*The Queen's Jewels*), and Suzy Menkes (*The Royal Jewels*).

The Lady Elizabeth

Elizabeth Angela Marguerite Bowes Lyon was born on 4 August 1900, but where remains a mystery. The Queen Mother herself is said not to know. Lord Glamis allowed seven weeks to pass before he drove into Hitchin from his estate at St Paul's, Walden Bury in Hertfordshire to register the birth of his newest daughter, so for years it was assumed that was where she was born. But at the time of Her Majesty's eightieth birthday her staff disclosed that it was London. No one knows precisely where and who would have thought future generations would be curious about the birthplace of the ninth child of the heir to the Earldom of Strathmore.

Two years later Elizabeth was joined in the nursery by a brother, David, from whom she was to become inseparable as the family moved between sylvan St Paul's, their London home in St James's Square, and Glamis Castle. In 1904 Elizabeth's father inherited the Earldom and she became the Lady Elizabeth. The new 14th Earl of Strathmore – Claud George Bowes Lyon – was an old-fashioned aristocrat in the best sense, unfailing in the discharge of his responsibilities as laird, kind, courteous, and sporting too, regularly turning out for the Glamis cricket XI.

Lady Strathmore shared her youngest daughter's zest for life, her gift for friendship, and a loathing of pretension. She brought her children up without frills, and they worshipped her for it. The daughter of the Reverend Charles Cavendish-Bentinck, a cousin of the Duke of Portland, she displayed an unstuffy Christian faith which she passed on to her daughter. A friend of the Queen Mother once remarked: 'I have never known her miss church on Sunday, even in the depths of Africa. She has been to some pretty erratic services, but it's all God to her.'

No Bowes Lyon child could escape its legacy of history. Lady Elizabeth learned early on that she was descended from King Robert the Bruce, and that a sixteenth-century Lady Glamis was

LEFT The Queen Mother arrives for an evening engagement.
She wears one of her grand, shimmering, formal gowns, designed in a style
reminiscent of those created to emphasise her regality
when she first became Queen.

burnt as a witch on the Castle Hill of Edinburgh. Macbeth, of course, was Thane of Glamis – and a much better King of Scots than Shakespeare gave him credit.

The sunlit years of an Edwardian childhood passed quickly. Lady Elizabeth raced her brother David up and down the witch's-hat towers of Glamis, or played hide and seek in the Walden Bury woodlands. Their mother dubbed them her two Benjamins. She learned to fly fish, to sew and cook. There were family sing-songs round the piano, a cheerful pleasure Lady Elizabeth imported into the royal family.

Ensconced in the background was the unflappable Clara Knight, a Hertfordshire farmer's daughter, who had been taken on as family nanny when she was seventeen and was known affectionately as Alah because her infant charges could not twist their tongues around Clara. And Alah she remained, becoming nanny to the baby Princess Elizabeth when her parents, then Duke and Duchess of York, toured Australia and New Zealand in 1927.

The five-year-old Lady Elizabeth met her future husband for the first time when they were both invited to a children's party. Sitting next to the agonisingly shy nine-year-old Prince Albert Frederick Arthur George, second son of the Prince and Princess of Wales, she removed the cherries from her cake, as a gesture of friendship, slipping them to his plate.

War with Germany was declared on Elizabeth's fourteenth birthday and Glamis was quickly turned into a military hospital. The Bowes Lyon sons joined their regiments, the fourth, Fergus, meeting death in action with the Black Watch at Loos in 1915. Lady Elizabeth became a hospital orderly. Seeing the results of bloody trench warfare every day for four years ensured she grew up rapidly. It was a sober training for a life of royal duty.

At St Paul's, Walden Bury, her parents' Hertfordshire home,
two-year-old Elizabeth Angela Marguerite poses on her birthday
for a local photographer. Round her neck is her first necklace,
a string of coral beads, which as Duchess of York she was to give
to her infant elder daughter, the Queen, who in turn passed
them on to her daughter, the Princess Royal.

The Queen Mother at nine.
A formal portrait taken at Glamis Castle in 1909.
Five years earlier she had become Lady Elizabeth Bowes Lyon
when her father, Lord Glamis, succeeded his father as 14th Earl of Strathmore,
becoming the owner of three ancestral homes, and 65,000 acres
in Scotland, County Durham, and Hertfordshire.

RIGHT *The scene captured on film by a visitor to Glamis in the summer of 1909.*
In the castle's great hall Lady Elizabeth plays the princess in sixteenth-century-style
fancy dress, partnered by her seven-year-old brother, David, in jester costume.
The children's dancing master, old Mr Neal, who had driven over from Forfar, looks on.

A Strathmore family group.
Back row: Fergus, killed in action with the Black Watch at Loos in 1915;
John, the second son, who married Fenella Hepburn-Stuart-Forbes-Trefusis; the Earl of Strathmore;
Mary, who married Baron Elphinstone; the eldest son, Patrick, who married Lady Dorothy Godolphin Osborne;
the third son, Alexander, who died in 1911, aged twenty-four.
Front row: Rose, the seventh child, who married Earl Granville;
Lady Strathmore with, on her knee, David, who became Sir David Bowes Lyon and married Rachel Spender-Clay;
Elizabeth (maybe encouraging her little brother to wriggle); and Michael, who married Elizabeth Cator.

An Edwardian afternoon. Elizabeth does the rounds with her brother David at a Glamis garden party.

Elizabeth with her mother and sister, Rose, at Glamis.
Rose had had a nursing training so was nurse-in-charge when the castle became a military hospital
in the Great War. Elizabeth acted as orderly. Her main preoccupation for the four years of the war
and its aftermath was the welfare of the wounded and convalescent. Over 1,500 soldiers
were nursed back to health at Glamis and many of them turned out to cheer
Lady Elizabeth when she was Duchess of York.

*The summer of 1920. Three months after the London ball at which the
Duke of York met Lady Elizabeth again for the first time since childhood, he visits Glamis.
The Duke gazes tentatively towards the camera over her right shoulder.
The following spring he proposed, but Elizabeth, who had misgivings about a future
lived in the limelight as a member of the royal family, turned him down.*

Lady Elizabeth at home in the garden of St Paul's, Walden Bury.
It is September 1921 and the Duke of York still nurtured hopes of making her a royal bride.
Earlier that summer he had visited Glamis again, where he was joined by his mother, Queen Mary,
a visit which confirmed the Queen's belief that her son had made the perfect choice.

RIGHT *That same summer at Walden Bury with her father, the 14th Earl of Strathmore.*

Royal Duchess

The lights of London, dimmed during four years of conflict, shone brightly again after the Armistice to illuminate a social scene far different from that of pre-war. Skirts became shorter, hair was cropped, and a heady mix of jazz and the cocktail gave birth to the bright young things.

Lady Elizabeth came out in the summer of 1919 when most of her contemporaries were determined to make up for lost time. But, despite turning many heads and hearts with her subtle Celtic colouring, her style remained just a little old fashioned . . . and has been so ever since.

She was described as 'the best little dancer in London', but she avoided night clubs and parties which broke up at dawn. At a ball given by Lord Farquhar, Edward VII's Master of the Household, at his house in Grosvenor Square three months before her twentieth birthday she again met the King's second son, then in his final term at Cambridge, and soon to be created Duke of York. Prince Albert, twenty-four, had served in the Royal Navy during the war, and saw action at Jutland. But from childhood he had suffered from a speech impediment which caused him to stammer, and this emphasised his reserve.

However, like Lady Elizabeth he was a good dancer, and soon he was partnering her. Enchanted, he resolved to woo and win her. He was invited to Glamis, twice proposed marriage and was twice turned down.

Lady Elizabeth was too sure of her own birthright to be dazzled by royalty, and had misgivings about surrendering her uncomplicated, informal privacy for a circumscribed life as a member of the royal family. Her father voiced a different concern, expressing 'grave doubts' about the Prince of Wales. He questioned whether the Prince would ever come to the throne, and predicted that, if he did, he might not last. 'Then where should we be?' he asked.

But whatever doubts Lady Elizabeth might have had, she overcame them in the Walden Bury woodland on 13 January 1923

LEFT *Lady Strathmore gave this framed miniature of her daughter to the Duke of York as a wedding present and he always kept it on his desk at the Royal Lodge. Lady Elizabeth wears the long string of pearls with pendant drop which appear time and again in pictures of her during this period.*

when she finally accepted the Duke's proposal. Overjoyed, the Duke sent a cryptic telegram to the King and Queen. It said simply: 'All right. Bertie.'

The view of society was recorded by Henry 'Chips' Channon, Conservative MP and socialite, who in his diary congratulated the Duke as 'the luckiest of men' and added: 'There is not a man in England today that doesn't envy him. The clubs are in gloom.'

The wedding was in Westminster Abbey the following April, and the bride set the tone of her future royal style by laying her bouquet on the Tomb of the Unknown Warrior, in memory of the war dead buried in the Flanders mud.

The new Duchess gave her husband not only love, and the security of a happy home, but she called in a speech therapist and together they cured his stammer. She beamed on everyone and they beamed back, dubbing her 'the smiling Duchess'. Princess Elizabeth was born in 1926, and Princess Margaret in 1930. The little Princesses became the darlings of the Empire. The young Yorks, carrying out a full programme of public engagements, were received with enthusiasm wherever they travelled.

But dynastic shadows were gathering. The Prince of Wales' latest affair, with American divorcee, Mrs Wallis Simpson, was coming to crisis point. The King, who had not long to live, declared: 'I pray to God that my eldest son will never marry and have children, and that nothing will come between Bertie and Lilibet and the throne.'

The King died on 20 January 1936, surrounded by his family. The Prince of Wales was proclaimed as Edward VIII and, with Mrs Simpson in the wings, the stage was set for the second great change in the life of the young woman born thirty-six years earlier as Elizabeth Bowes Lyon.

*This photograph of the Queen Mother as a young woman pretending to smoke a pipe
was, judging by the hat, taken in the 1920s. It was found, with 5000 other
royal photographs, hidden under a wooden cover, in the late Duke of Windsor's bath.
The Duke's chauffeur for more than twenty years, Gregoire Martin, was said to have
safeguarded the photographs in the bath to keep them from the prying eyes of visitors
to the Windsor house in Paris during the fourteen-year widowhood of the Duchess.
The pipe probably belonged to the Duke.
The Duchess kept boxes of Christmas cards from members of the royal family,
and the collection included several from the Queen Mother, indicating that her attitude
towards the exiles softened with the passing of the years.*

Lady Elizabeth leaves her parents' London home in Bruton Street, Mayfair, for her wedding in Westminster Abbey.
The Times *described the bride as 'gleaming with silver and veiled in old lace'.*
She chose Nottingham lace for her wedding train to boost the ailing British lace industry.

LEFT *An engagement study. On 15 January 1923 the Court Circular*
recorded the King and Queen's 'greatest pleasure' in announcing the betrothal.
The Duke wrote to Queen Mary: 'I know I am very lucky to have won her over at last.'

The bride and bridegroom leave Buckingham Palace for Waterloo Station
in an open carriage drawn by four greys for their honeymoon.
They were showered with rose petals made by the blind.

LEFT *The new Duchess of York posing with her husband*
for this official marriage photograph taken in Buckingham Palace.
The bride's dress, still lovingly preserved in layers of white tissue at Clarence House,
was of ivory chiffon moire, embroidered with silver thread and pearls, the sleeves
were lace. Her tulle veil was held in place with orange blossom and
two white roses – the white roses of York.

Putting at Polesden Lacey. They went on for the second part of the honeymoon to Glamis,
where the bride went down with whooping cough, and then Frogmore, close to Windsor Castle.

LEFT *The Duke and Duchess of York spent the first part of their honeymoon at Polesden Lacey, near Dorking,*
a house lent them by Mrs Ronald Greville, a leading figure in London society.

*First public duties. In the summer of 1923 the Duchess of York spent an afternoon
with a thousand East End children at Loughton, Essex, on the edge of Epping Forest.
The boys watch with critical interest as she knocks down a coconut in a side-show.
When sold for charity, the coconut raised £2.00, a respectable sum in 1923.*

RIGHT *The Duke and Duchess of York at Balmoral, where in September 1923
they joined the royal family for their annual summer holiday on Deeside.*

Proud parents. Princess Elizabeth, the present Queen, was born on 21 April 1926.

*Princess Elizabeth out for an airing with her nanny, the redoubtable Clara Knight,
who joined the Bowes Lyon family when Elizabeth was two years old.*

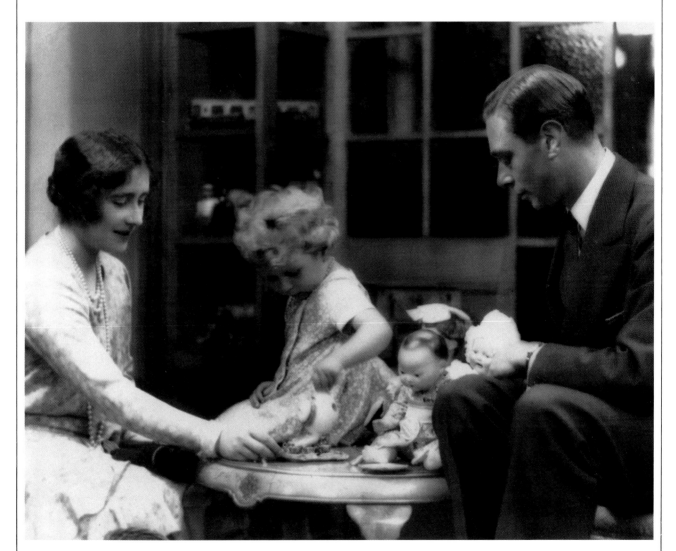

A doll's tea party.
The Duchess of York steadies the tray, while Princess Elizabeth pours the tea.
A nursery scene in July 1929. Princess Margaret was born in August 1930.

LEFT *The Duchess of York holds a smiling Princess Elizabeth.*
Soon they were to be parted when George V sent the Duke and Duchess
on an official visit to Australia and New Zealand.
The Princess was seven months old when her parents sailed away on HMS Renown
and fourteen months old when they returned. The Duchess was disconsolate
at having to leave her daughter behind.

*Souvenir of a royal progress. Thirteen studies in expression
of the Duchess of York taken when she and the Duke toured Australia in 1927.*

LEFT *Time off during the seven-month tour of Australia and New Zealand in 1927.
The Duchess of York lands an eight-pound rainbow trout at Lake Wanaka, South Island.
She has since fished all over the world, but her happiest times as an angler
have been spent on the glorious waters of the Dee at Balmoral, and further north
on the river Thurso, close to her beloved Castle of Mey in Caithness.*

March 1933. The Duchess of York opens the Frances Gray House in Ocean Street, Stepney, East London.

LEFT *The Duchess of York visits disabled ex-servicemen in May 1931*
and the following month tries her hand at a side-show while attending a garden party
for the Medical Benevolent Fund Guild.

Princess Elizabeth was five years old and Princess Margaret ten months
when they posed for this family group with their parents in June 1931.

RIGHT *St Paul's Cathedral, May 1935. The Duke and Duchess of York with the two Princesses*
at the service to commemorate the Silver Jubilee of King George V and Queen Mary.
The old King's health was uncertain, and he was to die the following January.

*The Duke and Duchess of York with nine-year-old Princess Elizabeth
at the Richmond Horse Show in 1935.*

RIGHT *Royal corgis begin to steal the scene as the Duke of York, watched by the Duchess,
plays with his daughters outside Y Bwthyn Bach, the miniature cottage in the grounds of Royal Lodge,
a gift to the Princesses from the people of Wales. A few months after this picture was taken
all their lives were to change completely.*

Her Majesty the Queen

J ust three weeks after bringing hope to the unemployed of the distressed South Wales valleys with his declaration that 'Something must be done', King Edward VIII surrendered his crown for love. He had been King for less than a year.

The weeks of uncertainty and conjecture for the heir presumptive and his family ended on 10 December 1936 with the King's abdication. In his nationwide broadcast the following day the former King pledged his allegiance to his younger brother and said, somewhat poignantly: 'He has one matchless blessing, enjoyed by so many of you and not bestowed on me – a happy home with his wife and children.' That night the future Duke of Windsor sailed for France and a life in exile. In his diary King George VI described 11 December as 'that dreadful day'.

The new Queen and Empress of India (the last) was in bed with influenza at the family's London home, 145 Piccadilly, as the last act of the abdication drama was played out. Philosophically, she told a member of her Household: 'We must take what is coming to us and make the best of it.' And she wrote to the Archbishop of Canterbury, Cosmo Lang: 'I can hardly now believe that we have been called to this tremendous task and the curious thing is that we are not afraid. I feel that God has enabled us to face the situation calmly.' But despite her outward tranquillity she was having to face the abrupt dislocation of her cherished family life. The serious misgivings which caused her to hesitate before accepting her husband's proposal of marriage thirteen years earlier had now become reality. She was bitter and disillusioned by her impulsive brother-in-law's desertion, and friends claim now that, although she mellowed somewhat towards his widow in the Duchess of Windsor's final years and went so far as to exchange Christmas cards and send her flowers, she never really forgave her for being the catalyst of the abdication.

LEFT *The coronation of King George VI and Queen Elizabeth on 12 May 1937. The new King and Queen with the princesses at Buckingham Palace after the ceremony.*

Elizabeth had become Queen at a period when the United Kingdom still confidently believed itself to be a great Imperial power and, describing her feelings to a friend in the month before her coronation, she talked about 'the intolerable honour'. Britain and the Empire had to be re-assured about the stability of the House of Windsor, and she and the King purposefully set out to restore the monarchy's dented image. At the same time they sought to revitalise it and make it relevant to the times.

With Queen Elizabeth's loving support the King was able to bring his great reserves of strength and ability to the responsibilities of monarchy. Together they successfully combined a popular image of majesty with an equally popular picture of a happy united family, a mirror reflection to which millions of other happy united families could relate.

Together they pulled off two diplomatically important coups. In 1938, in the face of the sabre-rattlings coming from Berlin, they made a state visit to France to re-emphasise Franco-British friendship. Hitler, watching a newsreel clip of the British Queen placing a solitary red poppy at the foot of a first world war memorial to the Australian dead, dubbed her 'the most dangerous woman in Europe'. Then, in May 1939, as the international situation worsened, they sailed for Canada and the USA. Again this visit, which did much to sway North American public opinion towards Britain at a crucial time in its history, was a tremendous success.

The King and Queen, who two-and-a-half years earlier had viewed their new roles with such reluctance, were now firmly established as world figures. But within months Britain was at war – a conflict which more than anything else was to forge the bond between monarchy and people. As death and destruction rained down from the skies Queen Elizabeth emerged with a new role – the Queen of the Blitz.

After his accession, King George VI and his family spend Christmas, as usual, at Sandringham.
Here they are on their way to King's Cross to board the royal train.
They were anxious to restore the royal family's public image of stability.

Queen Elizabeth is greeted by her mother-in-law, Queen Mary,
on Armistice Day, 11 November 1937. King George looks on.

Two months before their coronation the King and Queen went to Aintree
for the Grand National.

Portraits of royal ladies from the past by the artist Winterhalter
were the inspiration for these fairytale gowns of white and silver worn by the Queen
for the state visit to France in 1938. The designer Norman Hartnell
created a white collection because the Queen, mourning the death of her mother,
did not want to wear colours. The visit was both a diplomatic and fashion triumph.

Wrapped up against the Atlantic gales aboard the Empress of Australia
*on her way with the King to visit America and Canada. It is four months before the
outbreak of the second world war, and the visit is crucial for sealing
Anglo-American friendship and recognising Canada's importance to Britain
in the world conflict which is looming.*

RIGHT *The Queen in Calgary with members of an Indian tribe.
She is about to be shown a portrait of Queen Victoria.
The Queen Mother has returned to Canada many times since.
It is a case of mutual affection.*

The Queen, Princess Elizabeth and corgis.
The first two corgis, Dookie and Jane, joined the Royal Household in the early 1930s.

RIGHT *Duets at Buckingham Palace in 1939. The inevitable corgi stands guard.*

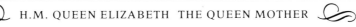

A Queen in War and Peace

As the victory bells pealed out over Britain in 1945 the people recalled with pride that their King and Queen had stayed put with them during the years of conflict, sharing their daily dangers and privations. Buckingham Palace was bombed nine times, and the experience prompted the Queen to make her most celebrated wartime response: 'I'm glad we've been bombed. It makes me feel I can look the East End in the face.'

With the defences of Europe crumbling before the German onslaught, the Palace became a headquarters for dispossessed foreign royalty. There was, however, in 1940, no question of retreat for the King and Queen, despite the very real threat of invasion.

The Princesses were 'evacuated' to the relative safety of Windsor Castle, while the Queen practised firing with rifle and revolver. To suggestions that her daughters should be sent to a refuge across the Atlantic, she replied: 'The children won't leave without me; I won't leave without the King, and the King will never leave.'

As the Luftwaffe attacks increased in ferocity, the King and Queen, together with the Prime Minister, Winston Churchill, became symbols of defiance. Within hours of a raid the Queen would appear with the King, picking her way in high heels through the smoke-blackened ruins to bring comfort to the bereaved and homeless.

The Queen insisted on looking her cheerful best, subscribing to the view that blackout colours, and flat heels did nothing for public morale, or for her own. Once when it was delicately suggested that she might dress more suitably for the aftermath of an air raid, she gave the unanswerable reply: 'They would wear their best dresses if they were coming to see me.'

The scenes she encountered were tragic, but while others around her broke down, she dared not show emotion. She poured out her pent up feelings in a letter to Queen Mary: 'I feel quite exhausted after seeing and hearing so much sadness, sorrow,

LEFT *On 7 September 1940 the Luftwaffe abandoned its offensive against RAF fighter stations and began its Blitz on London. The King and the Queen inspect a South London bomb-site five days later. She encountered heart-rending and horrific sights, but never once lost her self-control, although at times she must have been close to tears.*

heroism and magnificent spirit. The destruction is so awful, and the people so wonderful – they deserve a better world.'

Five years later she stood on the balcony of Buckingham Palace with the King, the Princesses and Churchill, while below them a surging mass of people celebrated the Allied victory. The war was over but it had left the King and Queen as drained as their people, who were now facing not a peace of plenty, but one of grim austerity.

In February 1947 the royal family made an official tour of South Africa and, two months after their return, speculation about a romance between Princess Elizabeth and Prince Philip of Greece was ended with the announcement of their betrothal. Their wedding, that November, was a welcome blaze of pageantry in a grey post-war world.

The King and Queen celebrated their silver wedding in April 1948, and their domestic joy was completed with the news that Princess Elizabeth was expecting a baby. But by the time Prince Charles was born, in November, the King was gravely ill. After the birth of Princess Anne, in August 1950, he had only eighteen months to live. The King died of cancer at Sandringham, aged fifty-six, on 6 February 1952 after a day's shooting.

His elder daughter became a Queen at twenty-five. Queen Elizabeth, the Queen Mother, as she was now to be known, became a widow at only fifty-one. She had been married for twenty-eight years to a husband who adored her. The King had evolved as a strong guiding force in their very happy marriage, and his widow appeared beyond consolation.

But, however deep her grief, retirement was not her style. She bought and set about restoring the Castle of Mey, set uncompromisingly on Scotland's north-easternmost point. It became a symbol of her own restoration to life – and to the road of service she and the King had set out upon almost three decades earlier.

RIGHT *The royal family at Buckingham Palace in May 1942.*
A basement became an air-raid shelter. The Queen made sure that food rationing was strictly observed and, in accordance with the fuel-saving poster campaign of the time, nobody took a bath with more than five inches of water in it.

Backs to the land.
The King and Queen visit volunteer agricultural workers hoeing a mangold field.
The Queen has sensibly abandoned her high heels for boots.

Raising morale in the early days of the war.
The King, in RAF uniform (he won his wings in 1919) and the Queen tour London's defences,
visiting sandbagged air-raid shelters and emergency centres. They both carry gas masks,
although the Queen's case is a softer, more feminine version.

Caught in an air raid in 1940.
The alert sounded while the King and Queen inspected this shelter
in a London Underground station. Thousands of Londoners took refuge underground
every night while the Blitz raged above them.

RIGHT *Surrounded by East Enders the Queen, followed by the King,*
emerges from an air-raid shelter inspection. It is August 1941.

Knitting for the troops in the grounds of the Royal Lodge, Windsor, in April 1940.
It is the eve of Princess Elizabeth's fourteenth birthday.
Princess Margaret is ten.

Summer 1941, at Windsor.
The Queen spurned suggestions that her daughters
should be sent to safety overseas.

Victory in Europe, 8 May 1945.
The royal family greet the crowds from the Buckingham Palace balcony.
The broken window behind is covered with black-out board and Princess Elizabeth is in her ATS uniform
as Number 230873 Second Subaltern Elizabeth Windsor. The princesses slipped out of the Palace
that evening to join the cheering crowds below.

LEFT *Huge crowds celebrating the end of the war in Europe – VE Day –*
surge towards the gates of Buckingham Palace to cheer the royal family
as they appear on the balcony.

The war has been over for almost eleven months,
but it had exhausted both King and Queen and the people they led.
The royal family had too few years of happiness left before the King's health collapsed.
Here they relax at Windsor.

The Queen protects herself from driving rain at the Royal Farm, Windsor,
which was playing host to an international conference of agricultural producers.
In May 1946 the country was struggling to get back onto its feet.

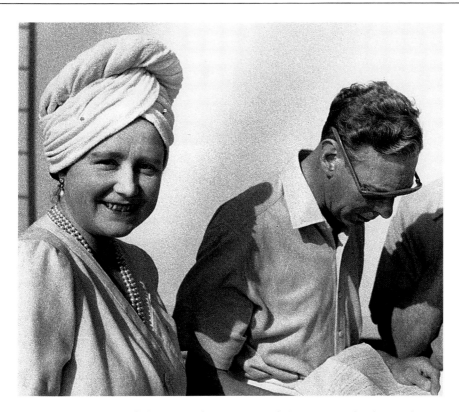

On board HMS Vanguard *the King and Queen are on their way to South Africa early in 1947.*
The visit had a double purpose: to unite the conflicting elements in South Africa
and to thank those who had contributed to the Allied victory.
The King, however, had deep misgivings about leaving Britain when it was in the grip
of one of its worse winters, with food and fuel in short supply.

The Queen and the princesses watch while the King presents an order to a Swazi Paramount Chief during the South African tour. The King's Equerry, Group Captain Peter Townsend, whose romance with Princess Margaret was to cause a bruising controversy eight years later, stands next to Princess Elizabeth.

RIGHT *Thousands lined the streets of Pietermaritzburg, Natal, to cheer as the King and Queen drove through the city. It was on this tour that the Queen made 'the worst mistake in my life'. She attacked a Zulu with her parasol when he darted from the crowd and grabbed the side of the car. It was not however an assassination attempt. He was merely trying to present Princess Elizabeth with a ten-shilling note for her twenty-first birthday.*

The scene during the thanksgiving service in St Paul's Cathedral.
After the morning pageantry the King and Queen were given a rousing reception
when they drove through twenty-two miles of London streets. The Queen in a broadcast
that evening spoke of 'our twenty-five years of happiness' and described the
sanctities of married life as the highest form of human fellowship.

LEFT *The King and Queen in the Blue Drawing Room at Buckingham Palace*
on the occasion of their Silver Wedding in April 1948.

*The Queen visits Cheshire in 1946 and encounters Mr Granville Barlow –
eighty-two-years-old and still working for the same Altrincham tool company.*

The King, accompanied by the Queen, presents Colours to the Parachute Regiment
at Aldershot in July 1950. Field Marshal Viscount Montgomery stands behind the King.
It is two weeks before the Queen's fiftieth birthday, when a Times *leader commented:*
'It would be impossible to over-estimate the reinforcement that the King
has derived from the serene and steady support of the Queen.'

The first grandchild. The Queen holds Prince Charles after his christening
at Buckingham Palace on 15 December 1948.

LEFT *Cecil Beaton conjures a romantic mood in an age of austerity*
when he photographs the Queen in a crinoline of black velvet, wearing the Regal Indian tiara,
the Crown Diamonds, and the Diamond Tassel brooch once owned by Queen Victoria.
It is 1948.

*Prince Charles waves to the crowd as he drives back to Buckingham Palace
with his grandmother and his aunt after watching the Trooping the Colour ceremony on
Horse Guards Parade in June 1951. Princess Elizabeth took the salute, deputising for the sick King,
whose doctors had diagnosed a 'catarrhal inflammation of the right lung'.*

*By November the King was well enough to be photographed with
the Queen, Prince Charles and Princess Anne on the Prince's third birthday.
It was the first photograph taken since the King's operation to remove a lung.*

The King's illness shows in his face as he talks with the Queen and Princess Margaret
at London Airport on 31 January 1952 before saying farewell to Princess Elizabeth and Prince Philip
who were leaving for Kenya on the first leg of a Commonwealth tour.
He died on 6 February.

RIGHT *Three mourning Queens at Westminster Hall –*
the wife, mother, and eldest daughter of King George VI await
the arrival of the coffin for his lying-in-state.

A Much Loved Royal Lady

Thirty-seven years ago, two day's after the King's funeral, the Queen Mother made a moving pledge to the nation: 'My only wish now is that I may be allowed to continue the work that we sought to do together.'

Now in her ninetieth year no-one could deny that that pledge has been honourably fulfilled. The painful road back started three months after her premature widowhood, in her beloved Scotland, when she inspected the 1st Battalion of the Black Watch on the eve of its departure for Korea. She had been the regiment's Colonel-in-Chief since her coronation, and her brother, Fergus, died fighting with it in the great war.

Within twelve months the Queen Mother was back in the royal round, sailing smilingly on, a constitutional fortress in shades of blue, pink, or turquoise, a hat with a wisp of veil, triple strand of pearls, and an assortment of diamond clips. It is the uniform in which she has travelled the world, and the length and breadth of the United Kingdom, swaying to the music of a steel band in Brixton, or causing a security flutter by mingling with the crowds in Ulster.

The years slip by, almost to a pre-ordained pattern. Her engagement diary has few gaps. There are fixtures which come round with the seasons; visits to her regiments, the Garter service at Windsor, spring forays to France and to Canada, with which she has a special relationship, every other year.

Then there are the days at the racecourse, visits to the ballet, opera, and galleries, and the jolly summer sojourns at the Castle of Mey with her family, friends and staff joining in sing-songs round the piano, followed by the occasional 'Okey Cokey' and 'The Dashing White Sergeant'.

Friends, and courtiers who have served her devotedly for years say that the Queen Mother is absolutely authentic and that there is little difference between her public and private image. She is

LEFT *The Queen Mother leaves Westminster Abbey after the coronation of Queen Elizabeth II on 2 June 1953. Her attendance at her elder daughter's crowning followed the precedent set by Queen Mary in 1937, when the old Queen, in a gesture of family solidarity, swept aside the tradition that Queen Dowagers should absent themselves from the coronation of their successors.*

kind, compassionate, but very strong, a no-nonsense woman; a criterion she applies as strictly to herself as to others. She is reluctant to accept illness, and regards aspirin as a dangerous drug!

A member of her close circle says that her enjoyment of people of every race, colour, age and background comes from the heart, keeping her 'young in spirit, happy and active'. And, she has no time for pomposity, intolerance, and unnecessary bureaucracy — traits her grandson, the Prince of Wales, has inherited.

Her ninetieth birthday year has been punctuated by super-latives, because, say her army of admirers, there is no other way to describe 'the most successful Queen Consort in history' who is simply 'our dear Queen Mum'.

Her life, like most people's, has had its mixture of personal joys and sorrows: sorrow over the death of the King; the ill-starred romance of Princess Margaret and Group Captain Peter Townsend, and the breakdown of Princess Margaret and the Princess Royal's marriages; joy in her six grandchildren and six great-grandchildren. But her greatest happiness and satisfaction must derive from the outstanding success of her daughter as Queen, continuing the House of Windsor's record of service, only briefly broken by the abdication of Edward VIII.

The Queen Mother is now the only survivor of the main participants in the abdication crisis. Future historians will give their verdict on her contribution to the stabilising of the British monarchy at that time, but even now, fifty-four years on, it must be recorded as vital.

And since then, during a period in world history, in which monarchies have not been in fashion, she has, by sheer force of personality, played a major role in popularising and guaranteeing our own British brand for generations to come. Her successors and the nation have cause to be grateful.

On the Buckingham Palace balcony following the return from the Abbey.
The Queen Mother turns to talk to her grandchildren, Prince Charles and Princess Anne.
You can almost hear her say: 'Isn't it exciting.'

A coronation balcony call for the royal family.
Princess Mary, the previous Princess Royal, is to the extreme left;
the Duke of Gloucester stands behind Prince Philip and the Queen Mother;
next to Princess Margaret are the young Prince Richard of Gloucester (the present Duke),
Prince William of Gloucester and Prince Michael of Kent, with Princess Marina,
Duchess of Kent, Princess Alexandra of Kent and the Duke of Kent behind.

The Queen Mother at her home in the far north, the Castle of Mey,
set on the wild coast of Caithness. The castle is very special to her.
She bought it early in her widowhood when she learnt it was to be abandoned.
It took nearly three years to restore, and now she spends part of August
there each year, keeping open house to family and friends.
She is pictured during her first stay at Mey in 1955.

The Queen Mother loves to dance –
particularly the Scottish dances she learnt in her youth.
Here she takes part in the eightsome reels
at a Caledonian Ball in May 1959.

The royal aviator.
The Queen Mother at the controls of a Comet jet airliner
over the French Alps in 1952, four months after the death of the King.
This picture was taken by Sir Miles Thomas, then chairman of British Overseas Airways,
who, in his autobiography twelve years later, described how the aircraft
nearly went out of control when an attempt was made to fly it
as fast as a Meteor, then the RAF's fastest jet.

The Queen Mother's 1958 Australian tour.
She is welcomed to the surf carnival at Manly Beach, Sydney,
by the President of the Surf Life-saving Association.

RIGHT *She said she wanted to meet the people of Australia*
and meet them she did. Huge crowds turned out to greet her everywhere she went
during the three-week visit. Here she boards the royal barge.

Saturday shopping in Ballater
during the royal family's Scottish holiday in Balmoral in September 1958.
The Queen Mother, with her two grandchildren Charles and Anne,
called in at a jeweller's, a stationer's and a toy shop.
Two months earlier the nine-year-old Prince had been created
Prince of Wales and a Knight of the Garter.

RIGHT *Over the garden fence.*
The Queen Mother chats to South Londoners
during a back-garden tour in July 1958 arranged by the London Gardens Society.
Every year she visits a different part of London to meet amateur gardeners
who share her love of gardens and gardening. Her enthusiasm began in childhood and
came to full bloom when she and the then Duke of York set themselves the task of creating
order and beauty from the wilderness threatening to engulf the Royal Lodge, Windsor,
which George V offered them as a grace and favour home in 1931.

The Queen Mother meets 'the Boys of the Old Brigade'
after reviewing the Founder's Day Parade at the Royal Hospital, Chelsea,
in June 1966.

RIGHT *The traditional Buckingham Palace balcony appearance*
following the Queen's Birthday Parade – Trooping the Colour – in June 1964.
The Queen holds three-month-old Prince Edward, while the Queen Mother
keeps a watchful eye on four-year-old Prince Andrew. Princess Marina, the Duke of Edinburgh
and the Princess Royal, the only daughter of George V and Queen Mary,
are also in the picture.

The Queen Mother at 10 Downing Street
for a lunch to celebrate the sixty-first birthday of Prime Minister, Sir Alec Douglas-Home,
who greets her at the door. It is July 1964.

*The royal family and foreign heads of state salute the funeral cortege
of Sir Winston Churchill from the steps of St Paul's Cathedral, 30 January 1965.
The Queen Mother stands with the Prince of Wales. Princess Marina and the Duke of Kent
stand behind Princess Margaret. Behind the Earl of Snowdon is the unmistakable figure of
General de Gaulle with, left, Prince Jean of Luxemburg. It was a particularly poignant
moment for the Queen Mother who, with Churchill and King George VI, provided an
inspiring national focus during the six years of the second world war.*

The Queen Mother greets the stars of the Royal Variety Performance, 1968.
The line-up includes Des O'Connor, Engelbert Humperdinck, and the Supremes.

LEFT *She takes her seat in the royal box at the Royal Opera House,*
Covent Garden, for a gala performance of Mozart's 'The Marriage of Figaro'.
The Queen Mother loves music, especially the more popular operas, while through her
friendship with the late Sir Frederick Ashton she has also become a ballet enthusiast.
And she delights in a really good musical play, like 'Me and My Girl' and 'The Sound of Music'.
Television favourites have included 'Yes, Minister', and 'Yes, Prime Minister',
together with other hits like 'Dad's Army' and 'Hancock's Half-Hour'.

The Queen Mother arrives at St George's Chapel, Windsor Castle,
for the annual service for members of the Order of the Garter, Britain's oldest order of chivalry.
George VI made her a Lady of the Garter soon after his accession to the throne in December 1936,
and the following year she was created a Lady of the Order of the Thistle,
the Scottish equivalent of the Garter.

RIGHT *Leaving St George's Chapel after the service which is always held in June,*
at the beginning of Ascot week. The Queen, who is Sovereign of the Order,
heads the procession of the Garter Knights down the hill from Windsor Castle,
The Queen Mother is invariably escorted by the Prince of Wales.

Straight from the horse's mouth.
The Queen Mother on the receiving end of a winning tip.

A Cecil Beaton portrait of the Queen Mother on her seventieth birthday.

The Queen Mother at the 1973 Derby (left), and at Epsom for the Oaks in 1965.
While the Queen favours the flat, the Queen Mother is undisputably the first lady of steeplechasing.
Her patronage has given the sport a previously lacking prestige, and in return
she has won the affection of enthusiasts that owes nothing to royal eminence.
She still turns out at Lingfield or Sandown, shod in waterproof, boots and wrapped up
against the rain and wind, a classic example of a consuming passion for the winter game.

*The Queen Mother casts an expert eye over one of the mounts of
the King's Troop Royal Horse Artillery in March 1987.*

LEFT *A rewarding pat for her ten-year-old gelding Isle-of-Man
in the unsaddling enclosure at Cheltenham after it finished third in the National Hunt
Two Mile Champion Steeple Chase Challenge Trophy on 15 March 1977.*

The Queen Mother as Lord Warden of the Cinque Ports
presiding over her Courts of Brotherhood and Guestling at Dover.
Her Majesty was appointed to this romantic but no longer taxing post in September 1978.
She is the 160th Lord Warden, and the first woman to have the job,
the origins of which stretch back into Anglo-Saxon history.
The Lord Warden is no longer expected to hold the narrow seas for the Crown,
nor fight England's sea battles, but the Queen Mother has inherited a legacy of
ancient beachcombing rights, including the privilege of claiming any flotsam or jetsam
washed up on the coasts within her jurisdiction. She no longer has any judicial or
administrative powers, but she is responsible for the burial of 'Fishes Royal'
stranded on the south-east coast – whales, porpoises and sturgeon.
She joked recently that she had so far not been billed
for any of these fishy last rites.

LEFT *With Princess Margaret and Princess Anne at the 1972 Royal Variety Performance.*

*With Earl Mountbatten and Princess Anne at Claridges
for the banquet hosted by King Carl Gustav of Sweden at the end of his State Visit
to Britain in July 1975. The King stands behind the Queen Mother.*

RIGHT *Arriving at the Royal Opera House, Covent Garden, with Princess Margaret,
for a gala to mark the Queen's Silver Jubilee in 1977.*

A tense moment during the April 1977 Badminton Horse Trials.
The Queen Mother, well wrapped against the cold, watches the cross-country section
of the annual Three-Day Event from a haycart.

RIGHT ABOVE *For years the Badminton trials meant a yearly pilgrimage to Gloucestershire*
for most members of the royal family, staying on the estate of the late Duke of Beaufort,
the Queen's Master of the Horse. Here at the 1972 trials the Queen Mother reflects on the form.
BELOW *Another Badminton cliff-hanger – the Queen Mother in 1972.*

As Patron of the Royal National Lifeboat Institution the Queen Mother
chats to crew members of the new Dover lifeboat in October 1979.

RIGHT *A spray of shamrock decorates the Queen Mother's rain cape*
when she presented shamrock to officers and men of the Irish Guards
parading on St Patrick's Day, March 1980. Her Majesty's see-through umbrella
has proved a boon to photographers, and it is typical of her consideration for others
that she should use one. Cameramen love her, especially the older generation of
Fleet Street men who recall the classic occasion when an over-zealous official
tried to push a press photographer out of her way, prompting her to remonstrate:
'Please don't do that. Mr — and I are old friends.'

*The family group at Buckingham Palace after the marriage of
the Prince and Princess of Wales in July 1981.*

LEFT *The Thanksgiving service at St Paul's Cathedral
for the Queen's Silver Jubilee, June 1977. The Queen Mother and Prince Andrew
being greeted on their arrival by the Archbishop of Canterbury,
Dr Robert Runcie.*

The Queen Mother, accompanied by the Prince of Wales,
rides in the 1902 state landau from Buckingham Palace to St Paul's Cathedral
to join representatives of the nation celebrating her eightieth birthday.
A crowd estimated to be anything up to two million cheered her on her way.
She was given a Sovereign's Escort of the Household Cavalry, and the Queen,
not wanting to upstage her mother, waived the Monarch's right to arrive last
at St Paul's and leave first. Inside the cathedral a specially commissioned banner
echoed the Queen Mother's spirit and philosophy, proclaiming in the words
of the fourteenth-century scholar and mystic, Dame Julian of Norwich:
'All shall be well, all manner of thing shall be well.'

In the White Drawing Room of Buckingham Palace
after the eightieth birthday service, with her six grandchildren, from the left,
Lady Sarah Armstrong-Jones, Viscount Linley, Prince Andrew, Prince Charles,
Prince Edward, Princess Anne.

Five years later – on her eighty-fifth birthday –
with the Prince of Wales, Princess Anne, Prince Andrew and Prince Edward.

LEFT *The scene in St Paul's Cathedral during the Queen Mother's*
eightieth birthday service of thanksgiving.

The Queen Mother chats to a young highlander at the 1982 Braemar Gathering.

The Queen Mother has a special word for the children when she goes walk-about
after being granted the Freedom of Windsor in 1981.

Prince Andrew, fifteen, on holiday from Gordonstoun,
gives his grandmother a seventy-fifth birthday present –
two pieces of pottery he made at school.

The Prince of Wales shows old-style gallantry
by kissing his grandmother's hand when they meet at the 1982 Chelsea Flower Show.

Mother and daughters – an informal eightieth birthday group.

The eighty-third birthday.
The Queen Mother with corgi in attendance
greets the crowd of well-wishers at the gates of Clarence House,
flanked by her daughters. Four of her grandchildren – the Prince of Wales,
Prince Edward, Viscount Linley and Lady Sarah Armstrong-Jones –
keep in the background.

The Queen Mother and her Guards. Every year she presents a
Battalion of the Irish Guards with shamrock to commemorate St Patrick's Day.
The Queen Mother is pictured here with the 1st Battalion at Chelsea Barracks in March 1981.
She is either Colonel-in-Chief, Honorary Colonel, or Commandant-in-Chief of
twenty-one regiments and service units, including all three women's services,
in Britain and the Commonwealth.

LEFT *The Queen Mother visits the 1st Battalion 51st Highland Volunteers at Perth in July 1986.*

*Acknowledging the greetings from the crowd outside Clarence House
on her eighty-sixth birthday. The Queen Mother was besieged by scores of
flower-clutching children, anxious to hand over their birthday tributes.*

'Just one —
An adman's dream coming true on the canals of Venice
during the Queen Mother's visit in October 1984.
Her Majesty accepts an ice-cream cornet from a cheeky gondolier
in a scene reminiscent of a certain television commercial.
The accompanying press photographers loved it, but
there was only an icy response from officials
who hurriedly replaced the ice-cream with a bouquet.

Formality and informality in birthday photography.
The Queen Mother relaxes in the garden of the Castle of Mey.
A study taken for her eighty-ninth birthday.

RIGHT *The Queen Mother at seventy-five. For this birthday picture Her Majesty*
wears the Garter Star and Riband, the Family Orders of George VI and the Queen,
and a necklace of diamonds and pearls, given by Queen Victoria's eldest son, the Prince of Wales,
to his bride, Princess Alexandra of Denmark. The tiara was made by Cartier
from South African diamonds owned by Edward VII.

On a recent five-day visit to Canada in July 1989
the Queen Mother arrived on Parliament Hill, Ottawa, riding in the same open car
which she and King George VI used fifty years earlier when they visited Ottawa in 1939.

LEFT *The Queen Mother at eighty in emerald green,*
a colour she does not often wear.

The Queen Mother was known as 'the smiling Duchess' when she was Duchess of York,
but the famous smile can vary from the gracious to the frankly mischievous.

The Queen Mother's style has changed little in twenty years.
The same loose-fitting dresses and coats, the same shell-shaped hats worn off the face
with a wisp of a veil, always in beautiful fabric, and soft, but eye-catching shades.
Sweet pea pink is a favourite colour but designers know that
anything in blue is an odds-on winner.

RIGHT *A birthday wave from the balcony of Clarence House.*

Walking by the sea with her corgis. A favourite pastime
when staying at Sandringham, the royal family's Norfolk estate.